Angels on Horseback
Lesley Saunders

smith|doorstop

Published 2017 by
smith|doorstop books
The Poetry Business
Bank Street Arts
32–40 Bank Street
Sheffield S1 2DS

Copyright © Lesley Saunders 2017
All Rights Reserved

ISBN 978-1-910367-79-7
Typeset by Utter
Printed by People for Print, Sheffield

smith|doorstop books are a member of Inpress:
www.inpressbooks.co.uk. Distributed by NBN International, Airport Business Centre, 10 Thornbury Road Plymouth PL6 7PP

The Poetry Business gratefully acknowledges the support of Arts Council England.

Contents

5	Night Lawn
6	Forensics
7	Autopsy
8	Gentleman's Relish
9	Strictly
10	Spooning
11	The Pavlovsk Seed Bank
12	The Four Corners
13	Day Dress
14	The Children's Children
15	Happy Pretty Thoughts
16	Elk-Ship
17	Angels on Horseback
18	Twelve Little Murders and a Bird Feeder
23	In Praise of Footbinding
24	The Shy Woman
25	Lilith
26	Adam
27	Rampions
28	Mitochondrial Eve
29	Acknowledgements

The reader is always overhearing a confession
– Jorie Graham

A bell rang for dinner
– Leonora Carrington, *The Sisters*

Night Lawn

And then it's all over, the ball that each girl
    shall go to, music and non-stop dancing
till she's legless, shoeless, hopelessly in love.

Only the night-scented jessamines, never smelt
    by the gardeners, and the lawn poor lawn
heel-pocked and moth-eaten by moonlight,

only between the trees a slight breathlessness
    leaning into itself, trying to keep a faint
flimsy of flesh pulled round its willowy bones,

only a screech-owl eyeing the secret lives
    of the small hours and the ghosts of shoes
mouse-like and papery, wag-wantons, tottergrass.

Forensics

> *The rags grew into garments, the garments were fitted on the figure*
> – Julian Hawthorne,
> the Leutgert Murder Case of 1857

When last seen, the suspect was wearing a red blouse.
Its thin silk clung to her breasts. Hiding the little knife
in the seam of her skirt, she turned and walked away

from the others, then disappeared deep into the wood where
the afternoon flared low and yellow on the limbs of trees.
In any good story this is where something must happen:

when last seen, the victim was wearing a red blouse.
Its thin silk clung to her breasts. Hiding the little knife
in the seam of her skirt, she turned and walked away

from the others, then disappeared deep into the wood where
the afternoon flared low and yellow on the limbs of trees.
The clothes were all folded neatly; no signs of struggle or

blood. The badness leaks out through their dreams,
sleeves lisp in the breeze; dresses grow swollen and stained.
In any good story this is where something will happen.

Autopsy

*Womanhouse with its sickly pink kitchen,
its woman trapped in the sheet-closet, its bride crashing into the wall...*
– Faith Wilding

See for yourself, the kitchenette just as she left it,
shirts on the ironing-board, bread in the oven,
nets neatly drawn across the pane in the door:

a practised performance, each detail perfected
by the workaday routines of make-do and mend,
kiss and make up, don't make a fuss – she knew

the score. Well, what more could she need?
Get down on your knees, then look slowly around
her TynieToy lair, the distressed chest-of-drawers,

the hairline crack in the mirror, the unkempt bed,
an overturned chair in the room where nothing
has happened. Picture the longings she scrawled

on the air with her lipstick, imagine poking your finger
through the hole in the wall of her heart, walking in
on a small-town killing, a nutshell study, a real living doll.

Gentleman's Relish

The goose won't squawk but the kitchen is witness,
its tabletop covered with bonbons and body-parts,

foie gras and forcemeat, fork buffet, cook's knife;
sees the dead-heads, chitterlings and chicken-livers,

tongue and milkteeth, claws and trotters, finger-food
à la maison, à la maman. Mother's ruin, slug and wallop,

done to a turn, oven-ready: breast is best. Quick,
look in the freezer, the linen-chest, the dog-house,

the walled-up fireplace, the wafer-space between. Wolf
it down, shovel it in, suck it up, lick the platter clean.

Strictly

*'up with my heels and down with my head,
this is the way to mould cockle-bread'*
              – trad.

for Susan

Mrs Bun the Baker – floury forearms, flowered pinny – is mad
about tango, traces an *ocho milonguero* with the toe of her slipper-sock
on the lino, imagines a fancy-man's hand the size of a ham
in the small of her back as the bandoneón sobs on

through another batch. She leans into the heat, sweat
trickling between the talced baps of her breasts
while she larraps the dough with her knuckles into butties,
stotties, cobs and bloomers; sets the loaves to rest

in their pans. As they doze and swell, she strokes the calf
of one plump leg with the ankle of the other, textbook stuff,
then hitches up her skirts and lunges low and slow,
fans herself and grabs the sink: her knees! But by teatime

she's mastered the *pasada*, the *mordida*, the *salida cruzada*
– so Mrs Bun puts on some slap, slams on her hat, makes a dash
for the bus, the studio lights, the gang of judges, the clapping crowd;
smiles as her bakery floats off on a cloud of giant pink meringue.

Spooning
   for Leon and Emma

Before beginning the spit-and-polish
of their new every morning chores

the pear-shape of her pleasure
rhymes perfectly with his silver fig,

their skilful finials ringing serviceably
together. No need for measuring

the soft heaps of hours and years:
here is ordinary treasure worn smooth

with baptisms and burials, the chrism
and vinegar in their bowl of days.

The Pavlovsk Seed Bank

During the blockade of Leningrad, twelve scientists died of starvation while protecting the institute's collection of edible tubers and seeds

In the dark, each is its own larder: pulse, pod,
stone, corm, bean – banquets biding their time.

Fine as sand or fat as babies, they're rich
with meat, sweeter than siege-bread. We eat

in dreams; by day we fast, our enzymes work
to waste us. Not one grain or lentil taken.

The Four Corners

But the bedlinen, worn thin by the press of skin and bone,
the caress of flesh, over the hazardous nights and years
of lives lived dream by broken dream, lay waiting

for the impassive fingers of mothers, who could glimpse
the pink of their own hands through the veil of threads:
sheets and pillow-casings and coverlets were turned sides

to middle, mended, made good for another pageant
of months and moons. Children hid in their canopies
as the whites hung and flapped on the line: sails and flags,

gellabiyahs, ghost-raiment. Then sudden scolding voices,
clouds bellying with rain and smuts. They'd learnt the drill,
the folk-dance: two pairs of hands at the corners, grasp

and pull, step briskly forward, meet and clasp, hold, fold.
Later in the hot dark they sprawl like puppies across the bed
while the backstitched hem prints a weal on their cheeks

like a seam where the soul might leave the body asleep,
attired in its fur and claws, to go wandering the earth:
the northwest passage, the silk route, a new Jerusalem.

Day Dress

'It is a grand work – it is truth – it brings something to the world'
– Mme. Grès, couturiere

for Laura

I've sewn *daughter* in pleats of dove silk jersey,
tacking invisible thread through old habits
of gather and fall, my small sharp-eyed needle

sheathed in a dozen under-thicknesses
of maternality that are pinned together
only by a moonlit plait of my silver hair

and the starburst brooch I've kept
of my mother's – the one she's wearing
in that photograph I insist is the same glamour

you shine with, the same mascara-dark waves,
and the nest-mirrors appliquéd on your sleeve.
When we've stopped excitedly remarking

on how tiny the female waist used to be worn,
you and I will turn and see how seamless
this moment radiates, the yards and yards of it,

you will touch its sunrays with the scented tips
of your expert gloves, you will fold it intricately
like a husband into your supple, intuitive skirts.

The Children's Children
for the grandsons

There's no-one to brush her yellow hair as Mother used to,
lost in reverie, with that faraway look. Gripping her chin
between long strong fingers Mother would drag at the roots,
humming a tune from some musical while rain whipped the lawn.
Dolly is wearing a skimpy muslin frock and a matinee jacket
hand-me-down; her arms are set at ten o'clock. The others loll around
in the cots where they've been thrown, crocked, blind in one eye,
nursing their love-bites; bear in a nappy, monkey propped
in front of the cackling TV. They wait their turn to be fed shakes
through a straw, for their syrup of figs, for their baby's bottle.
They can't help dribbling. Their smiles are stitched on.
At any moment the young guardians will rush in with their tongs.

Happy Pretty Thoughts

A hare looks at the moon.

The young can sleep anywhere,
against mama's breast, or ravelled
up in each other like kittens.
Clutching his grubby elephant,
in summer a little one will climb
on a windowsill, doze in the sun.

Window's left open. Slow drop
into slumber, gold hum of bees
in the flower-bed. The other child
looks on, smacking the doll's head
on the ground till its blue eyes close.
The young can sleep anywhere.

A hare can look at the moon.

Elk-Ship
for Malcolm

Half-stag half-ship, it is hiding in light
    like the dead of winter in midsummer
or the dark of a fin in the lake's glass.

The trees of its antlers are inscribed
    with fire, its ribs a ceremony of starving
and feasting, the old religion of sagas

and seafaring, mist-born shape-shifters:
    far from shore its oars go galloping,
ghost-herd through snow-deeps, leafless,

birdless, its frost-hoard glistening
    keener than pins. Beneath their deerskins
our bones are all ears for the hooves, the breakers.

Angels on Horseback

At the *thé dansant* she explains how the cancer
is eating her, melting her marrowbone to jelly.
She can smell herself, jugged hare, hung game.

All shaven and shorn, she sips echinacea
out of fine china, notices the hairline crack
in her cup. Perhaps she'll try a finger of toast,

a teaspoon of soup, a soupçon of sweet.
Nothing tastes good. She gets up to tango,
her scalp glistens softly under the lights, her legs

feel suddenly unsteady, thieved by the breeze,
oh, she's *vol au vent, mille-feuille, cabell d'àngel*.
She imagines her chemo-brain in its liquor, oyster

ready for shucking. The angels are coming.
Her dance-partner catches her fall, glides across
with the sushi, shimmies in the swim of her eyes.

Twelve Little Murders and a Bird Feeder

i. Eating People

Mouthing our hunger, stuffing ourselves with pinches of each other's thighs and cheeks – teeth and tongues testing for ripeness, getting to work on luscious flesh – we start at the extremities, going faster, greedier, till we reach the heart of the matter, and our lips, licking, lascivious, pout a mutual kiss. I could eat you, says mother to daughter.

ii. The Dollycollymoddle

How a thing becomes itself: wide-awake as shame, and faceless. How it is plaited from matted feathers, shreds of swear-words, red rubber bands, a small bone button. How something tiny there shining is the thin flight of its name, the way of a warrior, her own pleasure-pain machine sewn from the scabs of her cuts, her scat and spit, the draggle under her nails; how it will sit and mourn with her for days, days when she's breaking and tearing. Like a flower it burns a hole in the room, and the boys have seen. How her confiscation begins.

iii. Ana

Nothing white, nothing light and fluffy, count the number of bites you take, the number of times you chew. Eat in front of a mirror. As Tertullian reminds us, an emaciated body will more readily pass through the narrow gate, a light body will resurrect more rapidly and in the grave a wasted body will be preserved best. Nothing tastes as good as skinny feels. Friends will only get in the way. Food equals pain. Slim for Him.

iv. Onychophagia

I used to bite my nails. Neither bitter aloes nor bleeding nail-beds stopped me. Experts believe nail-biting to be associated with guilt and shame, often co-occurring with teeth-grinding, skin-picking, hair-pulling and pencil-chewing. Nail-biters typically suffer from *attention deficit hyperactivity disorder*, *oppositional defiant disorder*, *impulse control disorder* and/or *separation anxiety disorder*. Snorri Sturluson says the Naglfar is a ship made from the untrimmed finger- and toe-nails of the dead; it will break free from its moorings at the moment when the stars vanish from the sky, mountains fall asunder and all binds are snapped. You tell me.

v. Something from the Tooth Fairy

I can never resist bringing home the little clean skulls of voles or young rabbits that crouch, brittle as old leaves, in furrowed fields. Their loose teeth gather at the bottom of my pocket among broken bits of seashell and sweet-wrappers, still pearly, alive almost. Can I keep your tooth, I'll give you silver for it? It has blood in its cavity, a small red mouth shouting long after the wound in your gum has closed, reminding us who the tooth fairy is, why she must pay you in bright metal you will spend on earrings and lollipops.

vi. Dolls' Dinner

The flies were bad that summer. Bluebottles buzzed against window-panes, wrapped themselves in swags of spiders'-web. We found the black dots of their shit on sills, their pupae in cold cuts left on the larder shelf, in the dog's congealing breakfast. If ever we saw one caught on a flypaper, we'd stare in wonder at its enormous compound eyes, then crush its bristly body with the heel of a knife. *Calliphora vomitoria*. Blackberry jam round our dolls' mouths.

vii. House Party

Things liven up after dark: slender blades are laid against the flesh of freckled apricots, the cooling oven cracks like a gun, a tribe of cats thin as skewers look up with pale guiltless eyes from the carcass on the table. Salt's been thrown on the crimson stains. Afterwards, through the small hours, come drifts of unquiet air – perhaps the house has its ghosts after all. Or are they the familiars we'd meant to leave behind? (My mother, for instance, cuts my clothes to ribbons while I sleep.) Dreaming like lost souls, we reach out an arm to the walls, their moving lips, their fingers like scissors.

viii. Light Bites

Before becoming a living *sushi* platter, the person – usually a woman – is trained to lie down for hours without moving and to withstand prolonged exposure to chilled food. The *sushi* is arranged on sanitised leaves placed over her body, to prevent skin-to-fish contact. Guests may normally pick up their *sushi* only with chopsticks, although in some restaurants diners are permitted to nibble *norimaki* from the woman's nipples. Supine or prone, she's a dish, disappearing under a mound of *makimono, sashimi, tamagoyaki, wasabi,* garnished with *umeboshi* and *daikon*. In her mind she serves them other delicacies – rashers of their own hearts, diced brains, gelatinous eyes – on the plate of herself. Deep-fried and dipped in *shoyu*, they will taste meaty and mouthwatering, they will savour of *umami*, mother's milk.

ix. Junket

Watch Ganesha drink, see Mary weeping tears of blood: miraculous ducts and capillaries, arcane technology of well-springs, hidden pumps and pipes of mercy. Flocks of the faithful, whole cities in gridlock, mile-long queues to buy the god a pint of milk. Your face leaks salt and oil; now fake the creed, feed the frenzy.

x. Mass

I'm not evangelistic, it's what I do for a living, I'm like a small maggot working to clean out a huge wound – flesh and blood, gas and pus. I get paid in cakes and cheap sherry, just like the old times. They'd mould a midget out of stale bread, dib their fingernail in to make a mouth and eyes – a wee effigy of your dear old grandma or auntie after she passed away (god rest her immortal soul). And washed down with a swig of best bitter, so I heard. Well, like I say, as an occupation sin-eating had almost died out by the time I came into the world, what with the welfare state and all. These days I do a roaring trade. I eat the rich.

xi. Palaeo

It's obvious we're still hunter-gatherers, genetically speaking – our digestive system is designed for the thousands of years we were cavemen (and women, of course). So we should consume what our ancestors did: meat, fruit, nuts, fish, meat, insects, meat. Shun wheat like the plague, ban pulses, milk, cheese, butter, sugar, salt, yeast – that means no cupcakes, lady! Grow strong and lean, the best you can be. I think we should go further, actually, back to the old ways with words as well as food. Woe and dole, bane and bale, fret, flinch, chafe, sob, havoc – the ones we inflicted on the Neanderthals. Their brains were pea-sized and their teeth worn down to the gums from cracking bones, but at least they knew what they were eating.

xii. Gag (imambayıldı)

The imam fainted, and no wonder – all that olive oil: its unctuousness, its expense! Infallible, scholarly, authoritative, a knowledgeable theologian, pillar of society, man of God, great-great-great-great-grandson of the Prophet (peace be upon him), and exquisitely-mannered in other respects, the imam couldn't resist playing with his food when he was dining alone. He toyed with his *dilber dudağı* (beauty's lips), salivated over his *kız memesi kadayif* (young girl's breasts) and *kadın göbeği* (ladies' navels), and got stains down the front of his brocade caftans. One day he stuffed his face so full with these delicious body-parts that he could no longer speak. Indeed, he couldn't catch his breath; he choked and gagged; he flailed his arms and jerked his legs. His wife Fatima (the dutiful, the beautiful) came running at once, a glass of refreshing tea in her hand. She stood just outside the door. At last her husband grew silent, still. She eased her fingers between his slack jaws and hooked out the breasts, the navels, the honeyed pudenda. Sipping tea and pulling the gold silk thread from his coat she sewed her dismembered sisters back together. They never spoke of what happened – the imam had simply suffered a fatal apoplexy from over-eating.

xiii. Bird Feeder

I found a seed at the heart of the morning. I scooped its flesh with a bone spoon, then swallowed the stone. Finches flew out of my stiff arms. My blood ran green, I sprouted a thousand beckoning hands. I stood like that for a hundred years. In the dirt under my nails hatch the ten billion buddhas, grub-like and squirming.

In Praise of Footbinding
'Women are undergoing surgery to create perfect genitalia'
     – BBC News

The night is soft and dark as plums:

how beautiful the blossom in moonlight,
pale as rice grains.

How beautiful the vulvas of young girls
asleep in their narrow rooms.

In the morning there will be marriage-talk.
In the morning the cutting will begin.

This cut is called Opening Lotus Bud –
it will please the husband.

This, Undiscovered Pearl – choose it
also to stir pleasure.

And this, Silken Pavilion, and this, Perfect Peony,
will please greatly,

all the lovers will be delighted
with the sculpted vulvas of their brides

who until this moment had not known how much
the unsteady feet of their great-grandmothers

 – tiny, tiny – excited their husbands,
how the husbands were so delighted

that they wept.

The Shy Woman

Here is a woman whose bandages are cast-offs
from the time she was a cure-all for love-bite,
pharma for the gazed-at body. She hides her dancing

from male eyes, her veils are necessary, medicinal.
Here is a woman who chooses her words fastidiously,
her entire conversation is neutral, factual; designed

to deflect, even in his absence, the wronged melodies
her husband plays, the hands he lays on the world and her.
Here is a woman who asked for nothing, a head on a plate.

At each gate, she sheds a blouse, a skirt, her turban, tights,
scarves of skin, filters her piss through the seven sieves
of truthfulness. She beats the drum of abandonment.

Alone and stripped, her sister is waiting there in the flesh,
in the flowerless underworld, with lapis lazuli and lanterns.

Lilith

A woman is sewn of leaves
like a house is built of glass.
Turning her this way and that

you discover her texture
is neither fern nor feather
but what strikes you first is

the wild inescapable blue
how it palely inhabits her
how momentarily it pools

in the distance of her eyes
shining there like the frail ice
you know yourself made of.

Adam

This is not all his own work.
The blue that has hollowed
him out is virginal, like rain

not yet touched by the earth,
milky and lush with birdsong
and the soft slow hush

of suppressed engines. It's
as if he still can't quite believe
himself, the industry

and fieldwork of his ribs,
their alarming spaciousness
like the first draft of a person.

Rampions

Her lust is for rampions,
their fat flesh-like roots
white as a little one's wrists,
a passion that's sated only

by nightfall and her full-bellied
dreams. She'd stoop to theft
if she could, lamb's lettuce
from the rampant witch-garden,

the poor women's spell-salad,
round blond baby-fruit hidden
in quiet-leaved secretive places.
The sun is pale as moonlight

as the sickness rises. They bring
her buttermilk, comfort food.
She holds out her aching arms
to the crammed room, craving.

Mitochondrial Eve

Uninvited
I pull on my hat
of human hair; rattle
the back door, a small clatter
of wrist bones.
I've come such a way
for this christening,
little wizened chimp
in ivory lace
clawing at its mother.
Every wish is a curse.
The other mummers are mouthing
the hand-me-down stuff,
crayon lips, perfect pitch,
all the pretty fripperies, while I
shake out my spill of needles
and syringe of blood, lay
my memes, my implacable brood
in living plasm.
I'm the night-nurse
the old wives' tittle
the nanny's teat
the one they'll some day turn to,
my sleeping grubs
my aboriginal princesses.

Acknowledgements

'Angels on Horseback', 'Autopsy', 'Forensics', 'Gentleman's Relish', 'Happy Pretty Thoughts', 'Strictly', 'The Children's Children' and 'Twelve Little Murders and a Bird Feeder' were all written as part of a collaboration with the artist Susan Adams http://www.susan-adams.co.uk

'Adam' was first published (in a slightly different form) on a beermat, as winner of the Bradford on Avon *Poems on a Beermat* competition in 2014; 'In Praise of Footbinding' first appeared in *The North No 52,* spring 2014, and subsequently in *Hallelujah for 50ft Women: Poems About Women's Relationship to Their Bodies*, Raving Beauties anthology 2015*;* 'Rampions' first appeared in *The Walls Have Angels* published by Mulfran Press in 2014; 'The Four Corners' was first published in the St Cross College poetry anthology of the same name in 2015; 'The Shy Woman' was first published in *Mslexia* magazine in 2013.